A Diva's Guide to Employment

LAURA J SEGURA PHR

 Purse Size Paperback

*T*ake it from one fabulous Diva to another, if it weren't for my BFFs and networking, I would not be writing this guide and would not have obtained employment.

Thanks to all for your encouragement and your constant support. Every Diva must get beyond the grieving process of losing a job and move forward in a positive and constructive way.

Contents

Chapter One

THE DIVA'S
JOB-READY APPEARANCE

*L*et's face it, being unemployed is not good for your overall Diva appearance and style. Do you lack the funds to keep yourself looking great? If so, this is the time to be creative and think outside the box.

Clean out your closet and have a garage sale, or take some of the clothing you no longer wear to a consignment shop. You can also sell some of your designer bags on eBay. This will help you to generate some income and to keep up your Diva appearance and style.

Ask your BFF to come over and have a beauty day. Paint your nails and color your hair. Drink a bubbly beverage, and put on a mask or peel to give your beautiful Diva face a lift.

Finding a job is hard work, so enjoy pampering yourself. You deserve it!

If you need clothing for your interviews and money is an issue, check out your local consignment stores, thrift stores, or the clearance racks at the upscale stores. Know your budget, and stick to it. Once a fashionista, always a fashionista—just with a tighter budget.

Maintaining your appearance will help boost your confidence and get you ready to hit the pavement and network, network, network.

☞ APPEARANCE TIPS ☜

- A Diva always wears her makeup. You never know who you might run into.
- Keep your hair and nails stylish and up-to-date.
- Buy basic mix-and-match clothing.
- Have one pair of conservative black pumps.
- Dress your clothing up with accessories, such as a purse and scarf.

NOTE

Never wear too much bling, outrageously high heels, or very tight clothing. You must display the professional Diva that you are.

THE NETWORKING DIVA

*E*very Diva must be prepared to network. Do you have your generic business calling cards ready? Do the cards have a professional e-mail address and telephone number with a generic voice-mail? If not, immediately change your voice-mail. You can easily get cards made for low cost online, or make them yourself at home on your computer and printer.

Networking can be fun and exhausting at the same time, but enjoy yourself. Networking is how the majority of Divas are finding jobs in this economy. Remember, you're in control, so select what you know will be the best way to utilize your time and energy.

All Divas have a BFF they can network with. If not, make friends with someone that seems to be well connected. I'm sure you must have someone on your Facebook or LinkedIn account that you can network with.

There are two types of networking: social media and the old-school way of getting out of the house and meeting people.

With social media, there are a lot of ways to network and find employment. Just make sure your Facebook account is professional in appearance, without pictures showing a Diva's wild night out. It's okay to post on your account that you're looking for work.

Friends are the best referrals. In this job market, jobs can also be found on Twitter and LinkedIn. If you aren't technically savvy, ask your friends or a family member to help you. The Workforce Resource Center in your area or the local library may have classes to assist you.

Another option is to "Like" the company you're most interested in working for on Facebook. Also join networking professions and organizations on LinkedIn to keep on top of changes in your profession.

Remember, employers will be reviewing your social media accounts.

The old-school way of networking is some-times still the better way. Talk to your Diva friends, and tag along with them to chamber mix-ers and other events they attend for their job.

Volunteering is one of the most rewarding things you can do during your unemployment. It gets you out of the house, gives you a sense of purpose, and is something you can put on your résumé and talk about in your interview. It's also a great way to network and make new friends. It might even help you land an interview.

⇝ NETWORKING TIPS ⇜

- Put on the Diva charm. Show your confidence and be polite and respectful at all networking events.
- Work the room in Diva style by shaking hands and making eye contact.
- You don't need to hand out your cards to everyone. Be selective.
- Never overeat at events, and limit yourself to one delicious drink.

NOTE

You never know who your next boss or coworker may be, so if you're volunteering at an event, show your talent and work ethic, and do your best work. It just might land you a fabulous job.

Chapter Three

FABULOUS RÉSUMÉ TIPS

A résumé is a reflection or you, so make it fabulous. It's your personal calling card, your advertisement, your brochure, and your flyer—all in one. It's your personal marketing material and your key to landing an interview and a career.

Creating a résumé is not always easy, and it can be time consuming. In this market, you must create multiple résumés displaying your transferable skills for each position you apply for. The best way to do this is to study the job description and then create the résumé. If you're completing an online application, be sure to use the keywords of job skills listed and required for the job position. For the mature Diva, you don't need to list the year you graduated from high school or college on the résumé, and list jobs only from the past ten years.

When designing a résumé, make it easy for recruiters to find pertinent information by avoiding distracting visuals. You want the recruiter to locate the most relevant information immediately, such as your amazing skills, work experience, and education. On your résumé, keep the font the same, and don't overuse bullets. Try to limit your résumé to one or two pages.

There are many places you can go to get formats or assistance on a résumé and cover letter. And, yes, if they ask for a cover letter, they mean it.

When creating a cover letter, the important things to remember are addressing it to the hiring manager, making sure you list the title of the job position you're applying for, stating your desire for the position, and letting them know you look forward to hearing from them. Then don't forget to list your contact information.

On a separate page, list three business references and three personal references. Submit this list only when requested.

⤜ RESOURCES ⤛

- Go to your local Workforce Resource Center. The people there can assist with your job search and with your résumé and cover letter. They also provide computers, printers, photocopiers, and fax machines for you to use at no cost. Some resource centers may have funding for training and updating your work skills.

- Your local library may have computers for you to use for job searching and creating résumés.

- Your local community college may have a career center you can visit.

- Look online for résumé and cover letter templates

NOTE

Don't include a picture of yourself unless the employer asks for it. And use a professional color of paper. No hot pink! Contact your references, and let them know they may be getting calls.

Chapter Four

INTERVIEWING
WITH CLASS AND STYLE

*N*ow that you have an amazing résumé, let's look at how you can get an interview in six easy ways.

1. Ask your friends and family if they can help you get an interview with the company they work for. Get information about the company that can help you to prepare for an interview.

2. Twitter or e-mail your friends. Tell them what type of job you're looking for and the location you're willing to move or commute to.

3. Follow your favorite companies on Twitter. Look on their websites for job openings.

4. Recruiters and hiring managers search Facebook and LinkedIn for people to interview. Keep each account up-to-date.

5. Attend job fairs. Employers there will have a list of job openings and will usually conduct a mini-interview if you show interest in a position. So be prepared by dressing professionally, have several copies of your résumé with you, and turn on the Diva charm.

6. Sign up with a staffing agency. Working for an agency is a great way to get your foot in the door with a good company.

➤ INTERVIEWING TIPS ➤

- Dress like the fabulous professional Diva that you are, and be five to ten minutes early for the interview.

- Turn on the Diva charm to the front-desk receptionist, and make a good impression.

- Show up prepared to complete a job application. Have a copy of your amazing résumé.

- Research the company on the Internet; read its mission statement and takes notes for the interview.

- Be prepared for a panel or group interview. If it's a group interview, speak up and stand out in the crowd.

- Sell yourself. When the interviewer says, "Tell me about yourself," talk about your accomplishments, skills, and abilities, *not* about your childhood, family, or hobbies.

- Don't ask about the salary, benefits, or perks on the first interview—unless the interviewer brings it up.

- Show you're seriously interested in the job and in what the job responsibilities are.

- Don't lie, exaggerate, or brag about yourself. For all Divas I know, that can be difficult.
- Bring your list of references.
- The job interview is not the time or place to ask about job advancements or promotions. Focus on the job you're applying for.
- Be prepared to ask questions at the end of the interview, such as "What are the challenges in the job position?" or "Can you give me an example of what a typical day or week in the position is like?"

NOTE

Being positive and showing enthusiasm during the interview will make you stand out. Go to the interview showing that you own the job. Employers look for someone who's motivated and excited about working for them. Be prepared to have multiple interviews for the same job position. If they really like you, they may also consider you for another position within the company.

GET THAT JOB OFFER!

*A*fter the job interview, send a thank-you note to the hiring manager within two days. Keep it brief and sincere. This could give you an edge, especially if there is fierce competition between you and another applicant.

In a week, follow up with a telephone call. This will show that you're a persistent Diva who gets things done.

If a hiring manager states on the phone that the company hasn't made a decision yet, it's okay to ask, "Am I still a candidate for consideration?"

Then thank them for their time and consideration for the position.

Congratulations! If you receive a job offer over the phone, be sure to ask them about

---

- the starting pay and benefit package information,
- the location of the position,
- the work schedule,
- who you report to, and
- what you need to bring on the first day

Most employers follow up with an offer letter. Make sure you keep copies.

NOTE

Remember, my fellow Divas, it takes a few weeks to settle into a new job. Make friends, show initiative, and obey the rules.

Chapter Six

THE DIVA'S NOTES
and CONTACT LOG

Notes:_____

_____

_____

_____

_____

_____

_____

_____

CONTACT LOG

Date	Contact	Company/Job	Follow-up

Date	Contact	Company/Job	Follow-up

Date	Contact	Company/Job	Follow-up

Date	Contact	Company/Job	Follow-up

I hope you found this book useful and resourceful. You may have to endure a lot interviews before you find your fabulous job. But have fun, make friends, and enjoy your job-search adventure.

The End